TWELVE ROOMS

TWELVE ROOMS

A System of Containment
by J. A. Gucci

First edition, 2026

ISBN: 978-1-972788-19-6

Published by: Pressure System Press

CONTENTS

PART II: CRITICAL APPARATUS

PREFACE

These compositions initiate their inquiries within
the structural mechanics of the physical world.
Each room formalizes an observable system drawn
from geology, biology, optics, ecology, or
atmospheric science. Rather than offering
descriptive narratives of events, the poems isolate
the precise, localized thresholds where physical
transformation becomes visible through relational
shifts.

The volume is structured deliberately as twelve
distinct chambers of perception. Each entry
investigates a unique modality of observing change
via spatial relation, structural sequence, and
objective arrangement. By design, extensive
contextual data has been systematically omitted;
this minimalist reduction allows the underlying
continuity of each system to emerge completely
through its residual components.

These texts are not cryptographic puzzles
demanding hermeneutic decoding but formal
invitations to observe structural behavior.

HOW TO READ THIS BOOK

The reader is invited to identify what is explicitly present within the text before calculating what has been systematically omitted. Close attention should be directed to the manner in which one physical condition gives rise to another, how systemic boundaries shift, and how transformation becomes visible through the spatial and syntactic relationships between elements.

The poems do not provide expository explanations of the systems they present, nor do they invite metaphorical or symbolic interpretation. Instead, they offer a series of empirical coordinates from which the observer may reconstruct the continuous logic of the system.

We suggest returning to each room multiple times; new relational structures, geometric patterns, and systemic correspondences frequently clarify themselves through repeated, sustained observation.

"Nothing leaves unchanged.
What enters is contained."

Room I: Misplacement

Scraped cliffs
plucked
valley floor

dripping—
settled on the shore

stone
jagged smooth.

Room II: Uncertainty

Quivering photon —

double slit—

fringes.

Room III: Atmosphere

Blue
violet

green flash horizon—

apricot
red.

Room IV: Disturbance

Moon over pond
still

wind waft—

glints and glitter.

Room V: Re-seeing

Sun

glaring rocky wall
chink—

upside spruce
down.

Room VI: Transfer

Bone—
settled in silt—
soft,

squashed,
rain—

stone skull.

Room VII: Arrangement

Sun-dried pine
cracked cone

gust—

Aspen grove.

Room VIII: Trace

Dripping ice
slab

slumped in silt—
pothole lake.

Room IX: Alteration

Black billowing
plumes

glass shards
over scree

leek.

Room X: Saturation

A single parent
split

daughters
cleavage—

swollen tissues.

Room XI: Closure

Apricot sky

moon—
drifting on a glass lake

Room XII: No Self

Pooled in a basin
nestled in a valley

rising
towards the sun—

glittering white
crust.

APPENDIX: PRINCIPLES OF ABSOLUTE COMPOSITION

The compositions in this volume are generated within the formal parameters of **Absolute Composition**—a structural methodology that prioritizes invariant physical systems over subjective or confessional expression.

Each entry maps an explicit transformation achieved through spatial or linguistic containment. Within this framework, no element functions symbolically; nothing operates as a metaphorical substitute for an outside object. The structural system operates exclusively through the mechanics of what is physically present upon the page.

Structural Architecture
Each poem executes a rigorous, triadic movement
designed to track the lifecycle of a closed system:
A foundational condition is established and
contained. A defined boundary or threshold is
crossed, engaged, or modified. A final, resulting
state remains as structural residue. The
intermediate term marks the precise axis of
transformation, sustaining the systemic shift
without relying on narrative explanation.

Operational Dynamics
The constituent elements of each triad are drawn
from observable physical processes: pressure,
compression, entry, obstruction, accumulation,
division, and spatial dispersal. A contained system
does not remain static or neutral when disrupted;
what enters the boundary is inevitably altered, and
what remains is permanently changed.

Construction Methodology
The integrity of the composition is determined by
objective structure rather than thematic
interpretation. Language is stripped down to its
essential formal requirements:
No metaphorical language replaces the literal
object. No explanatory text supports the transitions
between states. Each line presents an isolated state;
the unmediated relation between these states
generates the final transformation.

Analytical Reading
To trace the mechanics of these systems, the reader
should explicitly locate three coordinates: what is
held at the origin, where the boundary threshold
occurs, and what structural residue remains after
the transition. Rather than inquiring into what the
text "means," the observer must track what is
contained, what crosses, and what results.

Systemic Recurrence
Across the macro-sequence of the volume, identical
systemic laws consistently recur: containment
generates pressure, entry generates disturbance,
division generates saturation, removal generates a
trace, and containment ultimately produces
absolute dissolution. The specific systems vary, but
the underlying structural architecture remains
constant.

Conditions of Stability
A composition achieves structural equilibrium
when the boundary is actively engaged, the
transformation is visually verifiable, and the form
does not depend on external explanation. If a
transition requires explanatory support, the system
has failed to sustain itself.

THE TWELVE SERIES: A PROJECT TAXONOMY

Each volume in the **Twelve Series** presents complex conceptual and historical systems through short, highly structured poems. Rather than describing external events, the texts function as formal models demonstrating how systems organize, interact, and evolve over time.

Each historical volume investigates a different civilization, utilizing an identical structural method to reveal the underlying lifecycles, thresholds, and operational laws that govern complex societal development.

Historiography

Twelve Clay Tablets (Mesopotamia)
Twelve Marble Questions (Greece)
Twelve Roman Thresholds (Rome)
Twelve Medieval Thresholds (Medieval World)

Creative Architecture

Twelve Small Windows
Twelve Loops
Twelve Mirrors
Twelve Rooms

Philosophical Inquiry

Twelve Iron Paradoxes

ABOUT THE AUTHOR

J. A. Gucci is a writer and theorist whose work investigates the intersections of system design, formalist structure, and the relationship between poetic form and empirical meaning. His books utilize constrained, highly structured methodologies to model how conceptual and historical systems form, stabilize, and transform over time.

COLOPHON

Twelve Rooms was composed in Palatino, an exceptionally legible serif typeface designed by Hermann Zapf in 1948 and modeled after the geometry of Italian Renaissance calligraphy.

The body text is set at 9-point type on a uniform 5.5 by 8.5 inch page layout. The typographic arrangement was engineered to balance structural compression with visual clarity, reflecting the formal compositional dynamics detailed throughout the text.

Designed, produced, and issued by Pressure System Press. Manufactured and printed in the United States of America.

www.ingramcontent.com/pod-product-compliance
Lightning Source LLC
Chambersburg PA
CBHW021349060726
47591CB00006B/2233